# Laos

# Everything You Need to Know

4

# Introduction to Laos

Welcome to the land of Laos, a captivating country nestled in the heart of Southeast Asia. As we embark on this journey together, let's dive into the essence of Laos, a nation often referred to as the "Land of a Million Elephants." Situated between Thailand, Vietnam, Cambodia, Myanmar, and China, Laos boasts a rich tapestry of history, culture, and natural beauty.

Bordered by the mighty Mekong River, Laos is a land of lush landscapes, from dense jungles to towering mountains. Its diverse terrain is home to a wealth of biodiversity, making it a haven for nature lovers and adventurers alike. But beyond its natural wonders, Laos holds a treasure trove of cultural heritage, shaped by centuries of history and tradition.

From ancient civilizations to colonial rule and modern development, Laos has undergone a complex evolution, leaving behind a legacy that is as diverse as it is resilient. Despite its tumultuous past, Laos has emerged as a peaceful and welcoming nation, eager to share its unique identity with the world.

At the heart of Laotian culture lies Theravada Buddhism, which permeates every aspect of daily life. Monks clad in saffron robes can be seen wandering the streets, while ornate temples dot the landscape, offering glimpses into a spiritual world that is both serene and profound.

But Laos is not just a land of temples and monks; it is also a land of vibrant traditions and festivals. From the lively boat races of the Boun Bang Fai festival to the solemn rituals of Boun That Luang, Laotian festivals offer a window into the soul of the nation, celebrating its heritage and community spirit.

And let's not forget about the culinary delights of Laos, where food is not just sustenance but a celebration of flavor and texture. From the ubiquitous sticky rice to the fiery delights of laap and tam mak hoong, Laotian cuisine is a testament to the country's rich agricultural heritage and diverse cultural influences.

As we journey deeper into the heart of Laos, we will uncover its hidden treasures and timeless wonders, from the ancient temples of Luang Prabang to the tranquil waters of the 4000 Islands. So, come along as we explore this enchanting land, where the past meets the present, and every corner holds a new adventure waiting to be discovered. Welcome to Laos.

# Geographical Overview: From the Mekong River to the Annamite Mountains

Nestled in the heart of Southeast Asia, Laos boasts a diverse and stunning geographical landscape that captivates visitors from around the world. At the center of this landscape lies the mighty Mekong River, a lifeline that not only defines the country's geography but also its culture and way of life. Flowing southward, the Mekong River snakes its way through Laos, serving as a vital source of sustenance for millions of people who rely on its waters for fishing, agriculture, and transportation.

To the west of the Mekong River, the landscape gives way to the rugged beauty of the Annamite Mountains, a sprawling range that stretches across the border between Laos and Vietnam. These ancient mountains are home to a rich diversity of flora and fauna, including rare and endangered species such as the Indochinese tiger and the saola, often referred to as the "Asian unicorn" due to its elusive nature.

As we journey eastward from the Annamite Mountains, we encounter the verdant plains and plateaus that dominate much of Laos' interior. These fertile lands are crisscrossed by rivers and streams, nourishing the lush vegetation that carpets the landscape and sustains the country's agricultural industry. From rice paddies to tea plantations, these fertile plains are the backbone of Laos' economy, providing livelihoods for millions of people.

In the southern reaches of the country, the landscape transforms once again, giving way to the vast wetlands of the Mekong River Delta. Here, a labyrinth of waterways and islands known as the 4000 Islands creates a unique and enchanting environment, where time seems to stand still and the pace of life slows to a tranquil rhythm.

In the north, the rugged terrain of the Laos-China border region offers a stark contrast to the gentle plains of the south. Here, towering peaks and deep valleys dominate the landscape, creating a haven for adventurous travelers seeking to explore the remote and untouched beauty of northern Laos.

But perhaps the most striking feature of Laos' geography is not its mountains or rivers, but rather the sense of serenity and tranquility that pervades the entire country. Whether wandering through the ancient temples of Luang Prabang or cruising along the tranquil waters of the Nam Ou River, visitors to Laos cannot help but be captivated by the country's natural beauty and timeless charm.

# A Glimpse into Laotian History: From Ancient Kingdoms to Colonial Rule

Embark with me on a journey through the annals of Laotian history, a rich tapestry woven with the threads of ancient kingdoms, colonial conquests, and struggles for independence. Our voyage begins in the mists of time, with the emergence of early civilizations along the fertile banks of the Mekong River. These early settlers, believed to be ancestors of present-day Laotian ethnic groups, laid the foundation for the vibrant culture and traditions that would come to define Laos.

By the 8th century, the region witnessed the rise of powerful kingdoms such as the Khmer Empire, which exerted significant influence over much of Southeast Asia, including parts of present-day Laos. However, it was during the 14th century that Laos truly came into its own with the establishment of the Lan Xang Kingdom, or "Land of a Million Elephants." Under the leadership of King Fa Ngum, Lan Xang expanded its territory and established itself as a dominant force in the region, encompassing parts of present-day Laos, Thailand, Cambodia, and Vietnam.

The golden age of Lan Xang saw the flourishing of art, architecture, and Buddhism, with the construction of magnificent temples and the spread of Theravada Buddhism throughout the kingdom. However, internal strife and external pressures from neighboring powers eventually led to the fragmentation of Lan Xang into three separate kingdoms: Luang Prabang, Vientiane, and Champasak.

The 19th century marked a period of upheaval and transformation for Laos as colonial powers vied for control over the region. In the late 19th century, Laos fell under French colonial rule as part of French Indochina, along with present-day Vietnam and Cambodia. Under French rule, Laos experienced significant social, economic, and political changes, including the introduction of cash crops such as rubber and coffee, the construction of infrastructure such as roads and railways, and the imposition of French administrative structures.

Despite resistance movements and nationalist uprisings, Laos remained under French control until World War II, when Japanese forces occupied the region. After the war, Laos briefly gained independence in 1945, only to be reoccupied by the French until 1954, when the Geneva Conference granted Laos full independence.

However, Laos' newfound independence was short-lived, as the country soon became embroiled in the geopolitical struggles of the Cold War era. The Vietnam War spilled over into Laos, with the country becoming a battleground for various factions, including the communist Pathet Lao, royalist forces, and American-backed troops. The conflict left a devastating legacy, with Laos suffering extensive bombing campaigns and widespread destruction.

In 1975, the Pathet Lao emerged victorious, establishing the Lao People's Democratic Republic and ushering in a period of communist rule that continues to this day. Despite the challenges of the past, Laos has emerged as a resilient and vibrant nation, eager to forge its own path forward while preserving the rich heritage and traditions that have shaped its history.

# The Path to Independence: Laos in the 20th Century

Let's delve into the tumultuous journey of Laos towards independence in the 20th century, a period marked by colonial rule, foreign occupation, and internal strife. As the century dawned, Laos found itself under the control of the French colonial empire, along with neighboring Vietnam and Cambodia, forming the collective entity known as French Indochina. Under French rule, Laos experienced significant socio-economic changes, with the introduction of cash crop agriculture, the construction of infrastructure, and the imposition of colonial administration.

However, the seeds of nationalism began to sprout in Laos during the early 20th century, as educated elites and intellectuals became increasingly disillusioned with French colonialism and inspired by the ideals of self-determination and independence. The emergence of nationalist movements such as the Lao Issara (Free Laos) sought to challenge French rule and assert Laotian sovereignty.

The outbreak of World War II in the 1940s provided an opportunity for Laos to assert its independence, as French colonial authority weakened in the face of Japanese occupation. In

1945, Laos briefly declared independence under the leadership of Prince Phetsarath, a prominent nationalist figure, but this newfound freedom was short-lived as French forces quickly reasserted control following the end of the war.

The post-war period saw Laos become embroiled in the broader geopolitical struggles of the Cold War era, as communist and anti-communist forces vied for influence in the region. The 1950s saw the emergence of the communist Pathet Lao movement, which sought to overthrow the French-backed monarchy and establish a socialist state. Meanwhile, the Royal Lao Government, supported by the United States, fought to maintain control over the country.

The Geneva Conference of 1954, which aimed to resolve the conflict in Indochina, resulted in the partitioning of Laos into two separate regions: the communist-controlled Pathet Lao in the north and the royalist government in the south. However, this division only exacerbated tensions and set the stage for further conflict.

The 1960s saw Laos become increasingly embroiled in the Vietnam War, as North Vietnamese forces used Laotian territory as a strategic supply route, leading to extensive bombing campaigns by the United States.

Despite international efforts to broker peace, including the signing of the 1962 Geneva Accords, which reaffirmed Laos' neutrality and territorial integrity, the country remained mired in conflict.

It wasn't until 1975 that Laos finally achieved full independence and unity, with the Pathet Lao emerging victorious and establishing the Lao People's Democratic Republic, a socialist state aligned with the communist bloc. Since then, Laos has undergone significant political and economic changes, but the legacy of its struggle for independence continues to shape the country's identity and trajectory into the 21st century.

# Modern Laos: Socio-Economic Development and Challenges

Let's take a deep dive into modern Laos, a country at a crossroads of socio-economic development and challenges. Since gaining independence in 1975, Laos has undergone significant changes, transitioning from a war-torn nation to one striving for progress and prosperity. The government has implemented various socio-economic policies aimed at improving the standard of living for its citizens and achieving sustainable development goals.

One of the key drivers of modern Laos' economy is its natural resources, particularly hydropower and mining. The country boasts abundant water resources, making it well-suited for hydropower generation, which has become a major source of revenue and energy for Laos. Additionally, mining of minerals such as copper and gold has attracted foreign investment and contributed to economic growth.

In recent years, Laos has experienced steady economic growth, with an average annual GDP growth rate of around 7%. However, this growth has been accompanied by persistent challenges, including income inequality, poverty, and limited access to basic services such as healthcare and education, particularly in rural areas.

The agricultural sector remains a significant contributor to Laos' economy, employing a large portion of the population and contributing to food security. However, the sector faces challenges such as low productivity, limited access to markets, and vulnerability to climate change and natural disasters.

In response to these challenges, the government has implemented various policies and initiatives aimed at promoting inclusive growth and sustainable development. Efforts have been made to improve infrastructure, expand access to education and healthcare, and promote entrepreneurship and innovation.

Tourism has also emerged as a key driver of economic growth in Laos, with the country's natural beauty, cultural heritage, and historical attractions attracting an increasing number of international visitors. However, the rapid growth of tourism has raised concerns about environmental degradation, cultural preservation, and the exploitation of local communities.

Despite its economic progress, Laos continues to face significant challenges, including governance issues, corruption, and limited access to justice. The country ranks low on various international indices measuring transparency, rule of law, and human rights, highlighting the need for continued reform and improvement.

In conclusion, modern Laos stands at a critical juncture, balancing the opportunities of economic development with the challenges of ensuring inclusivity, sustainability, and social justice. The path forward requires concerted efforts from the government, civil society, and the international community to address these challenges and build a brighter future for all Laotians.

# Exploring Laotian Culture: Traditions, Customs, and Festivals

Let's embark on a captivating journey through the vibrant tapestry of Laotian culture, where traditions, customs, and festivals weave together to create a rich and diverse tapestry that reflects the country's unique heritage and identity. At the heart of Laotian culture lies Theravada Buddhism, which serves as a guiding force in shaping daily life and social norms. Monks, clad in saffron robes, are revered members of society, and temples, adorned with intricate carvings and colorful murals, serve as spiritual sanctuaries and centers of community life.

Hospitality is a cornerstone of Laotian culture, with guests welcomed warmly into homes and offered food, drink, and conversation. Respect for elders and authority figures is deeply ingrained in Laotian society, and traditional hierarchical structures play a significant role in interpersonal relationships and social interactions.

Laotian cuisine is a culinary delight, characterized by its bold flavors, fresh ingredients, and diverse influences from neighboring countries. Sticky rice, served with almost every meal, is a staple of Laotian cuisine, while dishes such as laap (a minced meat salad), tam mak hoong (papaya salad), and khao soi (noodle soup) showcase the country's culinary diversity.

Festivals are an integral part of Laotian culture, with celebrations held throughout the year to mark religious, agricultural, and cultural events. One of the most significant festivals is Boun Bang Fai, or the Rocket Festival, celebrated in rural villages to herald the arrival of the rainy season. During the festival, elaborately decorated bamboo rockets are launched into the sky in hopes of bringing plentiful rainfall for the upcoming rice-growing season.

Another important festival is Boun That Luang, held at the iconic That Luang stupa in Vientiane, which celebrates the Buddhist relic housed within the temple grounds. The festival features colorful processions, traditional music and dance performances, and offerings of food and flowers to honor the Buddha.

The Lao New Year, or Boun Pi Mai, is perhaps the most widely celebrated festival in Laos, marking the beginning of the lunar new year with three days of festivities. Water plays a central role in the celebrations, with people dousing each other with water as a symbol of cleansing and renewal.

Traditional music and dance are integral parts of Laotian culture, with performances often accompanied by traditional instruments such as the khene (a bamboo mouth organ) and the saw (a bowed string instrument). Dance forms such as the lamvong, a traditional circle dance, and the khon, a masked dance drama, showcase the country's rich artistic heritage.

In conclusion, Laotian culture is a vibrant mosaic of traditions, customs, and festivals that reflect the country's rich history, religious beliefs, and cultural diversity. Exploring Laotian culture offers a glimpse into a world where ancient traditions thrive alongside modern influences, creating a tapestry of beauty, meaning, and tradition.

# Buddhism in Laos: The Spiritual Heart of the Nation

In Laos, Buddhism isn't just a religion; it's the spiritual heartbeat of the nation, pulsating through every aspect of Laotian life. Theravada Buddhism, the dominant form practiced in Laos, has deeply influenced the country's culture, customs, and social norms for centuries. Monks, revered as spiritual guides, play a central role in upholding Buddhist teachings and rituals, serving as pillars of wisdom and compassion within their communities.

Temples, or wats, are ubiquitous across Laos, dotting the landscape with their intricate architecture and serene beauty. These sacred spaces serve as places of worship, meditation, and community gathering, offering refuge from the hustle and bustle of daily life. Adorned with colorful murals, golden statues, and intricate carvings, Laotian temples are not only architectural marvels but also repositories of spiritual wisdom and cultural heritage. One of the most iconic symbols of Laotian Buddhism is the alms-giving ceremony, known as tak bat, where devout Buddhists offer food and alms to monks as they make their morning rounds. This daily ritual symbolizes the connection between laypeople and the monastic community, reinforcing the principles of generosity, compassion, and interdependence. Buddhist festivals are an integral part of Laotian religious life, providing opportunities for devotees to come together in celebration and reflection. Vesak, the most important Buddhist festival, commemorates the birth, enlightenment, and death of the Buddha, with elaborate processions, candlelit ceremonies, and merit-making activities held across the country.

The Buddhist concept of karma, the law of cause and effect, underpins Laotian beliefs about morality, ethics, and the cycle of life and death. Actions are believed to have consequences, shaping one's present and future existence, and the pursuit of virtuous deeds is seen as a pathway to enlightenment and liberation from suffering.

Beyond religious observance, Buddhist teachings permeate Laotian society, influencing attitudes towards life, death, and the pursuit of happiness. Concepts such as impermanence, non-attachment, and mindfulness are woven into the fabric of everyday life, guiding Laotians in their quest for spiritual fulfillment and inner peace.

Despite the challenges of modernity and globalization, Buddhism remains a vibrant and resilient force in Laos, offering solace, guidance, and inspiration to millions of devotees across the country. As the spiritual heart of the nation, Buddhism continues to shape the collective consciousness of Laotians, providing a source of strength, wisdom, and compassion in an ever-changing world.

# Ethnic Diversity: Understanding Laos' Multicultural Society

Laos' multicultural society is a rich tapestry woven with the threads of diverse ethnic groups, each contributing its unique traditions, languages, and customs to the country's vibrant mosaic of cultural heritage. While the Lao Loum, or lowland Lao, form the majority ethnic group and dominate the political and social landscape, Laos is also home to a multitude of ethnic minorities, collectively known as the Lao Theung (upland Lao) and Lao Soung (highland Lao).

The Lao Theung, comprising groups such as the Khmu, Hmong, and Akha, inhabit the mountainous regions of northern and central Laos, where they have maintained their distinct languages, traditions, and ways of life for centuries. These communities traditionally practiced subsistence agriculture, cultivating rice, maize, and other crops on hillside terraces, and relied on hunting, gathering, and fishing for sustenance.

The Lao Soung, including groups such as the Tai Dam, Tai Deng, and Tai Lu, reside primarily in the upland areas of northern and southern Laos, where they have preserved their unique cultural identities through their language, dress, and customs. Many of these ethnic groups are believed to have migrated to Laos from southern China and Vietnam centuries ago, bringing with them their own rich cultural traditions and practices.

Despite their diversity, Laos' ethnic groups share common bonds of kinship, community, and shared history, which are reflected in their social structures, religious beliefs, and traditional ceremonies. Kinship networks play a central role in Lao society, providing a support system for individuals and families and reinforcing social cohesion and solidarity.

Religion also plays a significant role in shaping the cultural identity of Laos' ethnic groups, with Theravada Buddhism serving as the predominant faith. However, many ethnic minorities also practice animism, shamanism, and other indigenous belief systems that predate the arrival of Buddhism in the region. These diverse religious practices coexist harmoniously, reflecting the country's pluralistic and tolerant approach to spirituality.

In recent years, efforts have been made to promote the cultural heritage and rights of Laos' ethnic minorities, including initiatives to preserve traditional languages, promote indigenous knowledge, and empower marginalized communities. However, challenges remain, including issues of poverty, access to education and healthcare, and cultural preservation in the face of modernization and globalization.

Overall, Laos' ethnic diversity is a source of strength and resilience, enriching the country's cultural tapestry and contributing to its vibrant and dynamic society. By embracing and celebrating this diversity, Laos can continue to build a more inclusive and prosperous future for all its citizens, regardless of ethnicity or background.

# Laotian Cuisine: Flavors and Influences from Southeast Asia

Let's take a tantalizing journey through the flavors and influences that shape Laotian cuisine, a culinary tradition steeped in history, culture, and the vibrant tapestry of Southeast Asian flavors. Laotian cuisine is characterized by its bold and aromatic dishes, which showcase a harmonious blend of fresh herbs, spices, and locally sourced ingredients.

At the heart of Laotian cuisine lies sticky rice, a staple food that serves as the foundation of many Laotian meals. Unlike in other Southeast Asian countries where rice is simply a side dish, in Laos, sticky rice takes center stage, often served in bamboo baskets and eaten with the hands. Its unique texture and flavor make it the perfect accompaniment to savory dishes and spicy dips.

Laotian cuisine is renowned for its use of fresh herbs and vegetables, which lend dishes their distinctive flavors and aromas. Common herbs and vegetables used in Laotian cooking include lemongrass, galangal, kaffir lime leaves, cilantro, and mint, which add brightness and depth to dishes.

Chili peppers are another key ingredient in Laotian cuisine, adding heat and complexity to many dishes. Whether dried, fresh, or in the form of chili paste, chili peppers are used liberally in Laotian cooking, giving dishes such as laap (a minced meat salad) and tam mak hoong (spicy papaya salad) their signature kick.

Influences from neighboring countries such as Thailand, Vietnam, and China are also evident in Laotian cuisine, reflecting centuries of cultural exchange and trade along the ancient Silk Road. Laotian dishes share similarities with Thai cuisine, such as the use of fish sauce, lime juice, and coconut milk, while also incorporating elements of Vietnamese cuisine, such as fresh spring rolls and noodle soups.

One of the most iconic dishes in Laotian cuisine is laap, a flavorful salad made with minced meat (usually chicken, beef, or fish) mixed with herbs, spices, and lime juice. Laap is often served alongside sticky rice and other accompaniments, making it a popular choice for communal meals and special occasions.

Another beloved dish is tam mak hoong, or spicy papaya salad, which combines shredded green papaya with chili peppers, lime juice, fish sauce, and a variety of other ingredients to create a refreshing and spicy salad that is both tangy and savory.

Desserts in Laos are often simple yet satisfying, with dishes such as khao tom (sweet sticky rice parcels) and nam van (coconut jelly) providing a sweet ending to a meal. Fruit also plays a prominent role in Laotian desserts, with tropical fruits such as mango, pineapple, and coconut featuring prominently in dishes such as fruit salads and smoothies.

In conclusion, Laotian cuisine is a celebration of flavors, textures, and aromas that reflect the country's rich culinary heritage and diverse cultural influences. Whether enjoying a steaming bowl of noodle soup at a street stall or savoring a traditional feast with friends and family, the flavors of Laotian cuisine never fail to delight the senses and nourish the soul.

# Wildlife of Laos: Biodiversity in the Heart of Indochina

Let's embark on an exhilarating journey through the wildlife of Laos, a country nestled in the heart of Indochina and home to a remarkable diversity of flora and fauna. From the dense jungles of the north to the lush wetlands of the south, Laos boasts a rich and varied landscape that provides habitats for an astounding array of species.

One of the most iconic residents of Laos' forests is the Asian elephant, revered as a symbol of strength and wisdom in Laotian culture. These majestic creatures can be found roaming the forests of northern Laos, where protected areas such as Nam Et-Phou Louey National Protected Area provide sanctuary for them and other endangered species.

Laos is also home to a diverse range of primates, including gibbons, langurs, and macaques, which swing through the treetops of its dense jungles. The country's forests are alive with the calls and chatter of these playful creatures, whose presence is a testament to the health and vitality of Laos' ecosystems.

In the rivers and wetlands of southern Laos, a different kind of wildlife thrives, including an array of fish, reptiles, and waterbirds. The Mekong River, which flows through the heart of the country, supports a rich aquatic ecosystem, with species such as the giant Mekong catfish, freshwater dolphins, and various species of turtles calling its waters home.

Birdwatchers will delight in the opportunity to spot rare and endemic species in Laos, including the elusive giant ibis, the colorful hornbill, and the graceful sarus crane. The country's forests and wetlands provide vital habitats for these and many other bird species, making Laos a paradise for avian enthusiasts.

Laos' forests are also home to a wealth of plant species, including towering hardwood trees, colorful orchids, and delicate ferns. These forests provide vital ecosystem services, including carbon sequestration, water purification, and soil stabilization, and are essential for the survival of countless species of animals and plants.

However, Laos' wildlife faces significant threats from habitat loss, poaching, and illegal wildlife trade. Deforestation, driven by agricultural expansion, logging, and infrastructure development, poses a grave threat to the country's forests and the species that depend on them for survival.

In response to these challenges, the government of Laos has implemented various conservation initiatives aimed at protecting its rich biodiversity and promoting sustainable development. Protected areas such as Nam Ha National Protected Area and Phou Khao Khouay National Protected Area provide sanctuary for endangered species and support local communities in managing their natural resources sustainably.

By raising awareness, strengthening law enforcement, and promoting sustainable land use practices, Laos is working to ensure that its wildlife continues to thrive for generations to come. As custodians of this rich natural heritage, it is incumbent upon all of us to protect and preserve the wildlife of Laos for future generations to enjoy.

# Exploring the Great Outdoors: National Parks and Ecotourism

Let's embark on an exhilarating journey into the great outdoors of Laos, where national parks and ecotourism offer opportunities for adventure, exploration, and connection with nature. Laos is blessed with a diverse and stunning natural landscape, from lush jungles and towering mountains to pristine rivers and tranquil wetlands. The country's national parks, protected areas, and ecotourism initiatives provide visitors with unique opportunities to experience the beauty and biodiversity of Laos while supporting conservation efforts and sustainable development.

One of the crown jewels of Laos' national park system is Nam Et-Phou Louey National Protected Area, located in the northern part of the country. This expansive protected area is home to a remarkable array of wildlife, including Asian elephants, clouded leopards, and rare species such as the saola and Indochinese tiger. Visitors to Nam Et-Phou Louey can embark on guided trekking tours, wildlife safaris, and boat trips, offering opportunities to spot wildlife in their natural habitat while learning about conservation efforts and local livelihoods.

Another must-visit destination for nature lovers is Phou Khao Khouay National Protected Area, located just outside the capital city of Vientiane. This biodiverse region is home to dense forests, scenic waterfalls, and abundant wildlife, making it a popular destination for hiking, birdwatching, and nature photography. Visitors to Phou Khao Khouay can explore the park's network of trails, visit traditional villages, and take part in community-based ecotourism initiatives that support local communities and conservation efforts.

In southern Laos, the 4000 Islands region offers a unique and enchanting landscape of riverine islands, wetlands, and waterfalls. This ecologically rich area is home to rare species such as the Irrawaddy dolphin and the giant catfish, as well as a variety of migratory birds and aquatic plants. Visitors to the 4000 Islands can explore the region by boat, kayak, or bicycle, visiting traditional fishing villages, waterfalls, and conservation areas along the way.

Ecotourism initiatives in Laos are not only about experiencing nature but also about supporting local communities and preserving cultural heritage. Many ecotourism projects in Laos are community-based, providing opportunities for local villagers to benefit from tourism while preserving their traditional way of life and natural resources. Whether staying in homestays, participating in cultural activities, or purchasing handmade crafts, visitors to Laos can directly contribute to local economies and conservation efforts.

Overall, exploring the great outdoors of Laos offers a chance to reconnect with nature, discover hidden gems, and support conservation efforts that are vital for the preservation of the country's natural heritage. By embracing ecotourism and sustainable travel practices, visitors can play a crucial role in protecting Laos' diverse ecosystems and ensuring a brighter future for generations to come.

# Luang Prabang: Jewel of the Mekong and UNESCO World Heritage Site

Welcome to Luang Prabang, the enchanting jewel of the Mekong River and a UNESCO World Heritage Site that beckons travelers with its timeless charm and rich cultural heritage. Nestled in the lush mountains of northern Laos, Luang Prabang is a city steeped in history, spirituality, and natural beauty, where ancient temples, colonial architecture, and vibrant markets converge to create a truly unforgettable experience.

At the heart of Luang Prabang lies its spiritual soul, embodied by the city's magnificent temples and monasteries. The historic center of Luang Prabang is home to over 30 temples, including the iconic Wat Xieng Thong, with its dazzling golden facades and intricate carvings, and the serene Wat Mai, known for its exquisite murals and gilded interiors. These sacred sites are not only architectural marvels but also spiritual sanctuaries, where Buddhist monks gather for prayer, meditation, and ritual ceremonies.

In addition to its temples, Luang Prabang is also renowned for its colonial-era architecture, which reflects the city's rich history as a former royal capital and French colonial outpost. Strolling through the streets of Luang Prabang, visitors will encounter charming French villas, colonial-era mansions, and quaint shopfronts, all of which add to the city's unique charm and ambiance.

One of the highlights of any visit to Luang Prabang is the city's vibrant and colorful markets, where locals gather to buy and sell fresh produce, handicrafts, and textiles. The morning market, held daily along the main thoroughfare, offers a feast for the senses, with vendors selling everything from exotic fruits and vegetables to handmade souvenirs and traditional Lao textiles.

For nature lovers, Luang Prabang offers plenty of opportunities to explore the natural beauty of northern Laos. The nearby Kuang Si Falls, with their turquoise pools and cascading waterfalls, are a popular destination for swimming, picnicking, and hiking, while the tranquil waters of the Mekong River provide a peaceful backdrop for boat cruises and sunset views.

As a UNESCO World Heritage Site, Luang Prabang is committed to preserving its cultural and natural heritage for future generations to enjoy. Efforts to conserve the city's historic architecture, protect its natural resources, and promote sustainable tourism have earned Luang

Prabang recognition as one of the most well-preserved and environmentally conscious destinations in Southeast Asia.

In conclusion, Luang Prabang is much more than just a city; it is a living testament to Laos' rich history, cultural diversity, and natural beauty. Whether exploring its ancient temples, wandering through its charming streets, or immersing oneself in its vibrant markets, visitors to Luang Prabang are sure to be captivated by the city's timeless allure and warm hospitality.

# Vientiane: The Capital City and Its Historic Charms

Welcome to Vientiane, the capital city of Laos, where history, culture, and modernity blend seamlessly to create a vibrant and dynamic urban landscape. Situated on the banks of the mighty Mekong River, Vientiane is a city steeped in history, with a rich cultural heritage that dates back centuries. From ancient temples and colonial architecture to bustling markets and lively nightlife, Vientiane offers visitors a fascinating glimpse into the heart and soul of Laos.

At the heart of Vientiane lies its historic old town, where ancient temples and monuments stand as testament to the city's illustrious past. Wat Si Saket, the oldest temple in Vientiane, is renowned for its thousands of Buddha statues, while the nearby Wat Si Muang is believed to house the spirit of a local woman who sacrificed herself during the construction of the temple.

Vientiane's colonial legacy is evident in its architecture, with French colonial buildings dotting the cityscape alongside traditional Lao structures. The Presidential Palace, once the residence of the French governor-general, is now a museum that offers insights into Laos' colonial history, while the Patuxai, a monumental arch inspired by the Arc de Triomphe in Paris, stands as a symbol of Laotian independence.

39

For those seeking a taste of local culture, Vientiane's markets are a treasure trove of sights, sounds, and smells. The bustling morning market offers an array of fresh produce, textiles, and handicrafts, while the night market comes alive with street food stalls, live music, and traditional performances. Visitors can sample local delicacies such as khao piak sen (rice noodle soup) and sai oua (spicy sausage), or browse handmade crafts such as silk scarves and silver jewelry. Despite its modernization and development, Vientiane retains a relaxed and laid-back atmosphere that is characteristic of Laotian culture. Visitors will find plenty of opportunities to unwind and relax, whether sipping coffee at a riverside cafe, taking a leisurely stroll along the Mekong promenade, or watching the sunset from the banks of the river. In recent years, Vientiane has seen rapid growth and development, with new hotels, restaurants, and infrastructure projects transforming the city's skyline. However, efforts have been made to preserve the city's historic charm and cultural heritage, with strict regulations in place to protect its ancient monuments and landmarks.

In conclusion, Vientiane is a city of contrasts, where ancient traditions and modernity coexist harmoniously to create a unique and captivating urban experience. Whether exploring its historic temples, sampling its culinary delights, or simply soaking in the laid-back vibe, visitors to Vientiane are sure to be enchanted by the city's timeless charm and warm hospitality.

# Pakse: Gateway to the South and Bolaven Plateau

Welcome to Pakse, the bustling gateway to southern Laos and the gateway to the breathtaking Bolaven Plateau. Situated on the banks of the Mekong River, Pakse serves as a hub for travelers exploring the scenic wonders of southern Laos, including the majestic waterfalls, lush jungles, and vibrant cultural heritage of the Bolaven Plateau.

Pakse itself is a vibrant and cosmopolitan city, with a lively riverfront promenade, bustling markets, and a rich culinary scene that reflects the diverse influences of Lao, Thai, and Vietnamese cuisines. Visitors can explore the city's historic landmarks, such as the Wat Luang and Wat Phou Salao temples, which offer panoramic views of the city and the Mekong River.

One of the main attractions of Pakse is its proximity to the Bolaven Plateau, a fertile upland region renowned for its stunning natural beauty and rich agricultural heritage. The plateau is home to lush forests, cascading waterfalls, and vast coffee plantations, making it a paradise for outdoor enthusiasts, nature lovers, and coffee aficionados alike.

One of the highlights of any visit to the Bolaven Plateau is the chance to explore its spectacular waterfalls, including the iconic Tad Fane, Tad

Yuang, and Tad Lo falls. These majestic cascades plunge into verdant valleys, creating a mesmerizing spectacle that is not to be missed.

In addition to its natural beauty, the Bolaven Plateau is also known for its thriving coffee industry, with small-scale farmers cultivating some of the finest Arabica beans in the region. Visitors to the plateau can learn about the coffee production process, sample freshly brewed coffee, and purchase locally sourced beans to take home as souvenirs.

For those seeking adventure, the Bolaven Plateau offers a variety of outdoor activities, including trekking, mountain biking, and elephant trekking. Guided tours are available for those looking to explore the plateau's hidden gems and discover its rich cultural heritage, including traditional Lao villages, ethnic minority communities, and ancient temples.

Despite its growing popularity as a tourist destination, the Bolaven Plateau remains relatively untouched by mass tourism, offering visitors a peaceful and authentic experience amidst breathtaking natural surroundings. Whether exploring its waterfalls, savoring its coffee, or immersing oneself in its vibrant culture, a visit to the Bolaven Plateau is sure to be a memorable and rewarding experience.

# Savannakhet: A Blend of Colonial Architecture and Lao Traditions

Welcome to Savannakhet, a city that embodies the rich cultural heritage and architectural charm of Laos, where colonial-era buildings stand side by side with traditional Lao temples and monuments. Situated on the banks of the Mekong River, Savannakhet is the second-largest city in Laos and a melting pot of cultural influences, blending French colonial architecture with Lao traditions to create a unique and captivating urban landscape.

The historic center of Savannakhet is a treasure trove of colonial-era buildings, with stately mansions, government offices, and commercial buildings dating back to the French colonial period. The city's French legacy is evident in its architecture, with elegant facades, wrought-iron balconies, and ornate detailing that harken back to a bygone era of European influence.

In addition to its colonial heritage, Savannakhet is also home to a wealth of traditional Lao temples and monuments, which reflect the city's deep-rooted spiritual and cultural traditions. Wat Sainyaphum, one of the oldest temples in Savannakhet, is renowned for its striking red-and-gold facade and ornate carvings, while the

That Ing Hang stupa is a sacred pilgrimage site for Buddhists from across the country.

One of the highlights of any visit to Savannakhet is the chance to explore its vibrant markets, where locals gather to buy and sell fresh produce, handicrafts, and textiles. The bustling morning market offers an array of colorful fruits, vegetables, and spices, while the night market comes alive with street food stalls, live music, and cultural performances.

Savannakhet's cultural heritage is also celebrated through its festivals and events, which showcase traditional music, dance, and cuisine. The annual Boat Racing Festival, held on the Mekong River, is a highlight of the city's social calendar, featuring colorful boat races, religious ceremonies, and lively festivities that attract visitors from near and far.

Despite its rich history and cultural significance, Savannakhet remains relatively undiscovered by tourists, offering visitors a chance to experience authentic Lao culture and hospitality away from the crowds. Whether exploring its historic landmarks, sampling its culinary delights, or simply soaking in its laid-back vibe, a visit to Savannakhet is sure to leave a lasting impression on travelers seeking to uncover the hidden gems of Laos.

# The Plain of Jars: Mystery and History in Northern Laos

Welcome to the enigmatic Plain of Jars, a mysterious archaeological site shrouded in history and intrigue in northern Laos. Spread across the rugged landscape of Xieng Khouang Province, the Plain of Jars is home to thousands of ancient stone jars scattered across the countryside, each weighing several tons and dating back over 2,000 years. These massive jars, carved from sandstone and granite, range in size from small urns to towering monoliths, with some reaching heights of up to three meters.

The origins of the Plain of Jars remain a subject of debate among archaeologists and historians, with theories ranging from burial sites to ritualistic ceremonies to ancient funerary practices. One prevailing hypothesis suggests that the jars were used for secondary burial rituals, with bodies being placed inside the jars after decomposition to facilitate the journey of the soul to the afterlife. Another theory posits that the jars were used to collect rainwater for use during dry seasons or as part of agricultural rituals to ensure bountiful harvests.

Despite centuries of speculation and study, many questions about the Plain of Jars remain unanswered, adding to its allure and mystique. The site's remote location, rugged terrain, and lack of extensive excavation have contributed to its status as one of the most intriguing archaeological mysteries in Southeast Asia. In addition to its archaeological significance, the Plain of Jars is also steeped in history, with the region bearing witness to centuries of conflict, conquest, and cultural exchange. During the Vietnam War, the Plain of Jars was heavily bombed by American forces, leaving behind craters and unexploded ordnance that continue to pose a threat to local communities to this day. Efforts to clear the area of landmines and unexploded bombs have been ongoing, allowing visitors to safely explore the site and learn about its history and significance. In recent years, the Plain of Jars has emerged as a popular tourist destination, attracting visitors from around the world eager to unravel its mysteries and explore its ancient wonders. Guided tours are available for those looking to learn more about the site's history and archaeological significance, with knowledgeable guides providing insights into the culture, traditions, and beliefs of ancient civilizations that once inhabited the region.

Despite its remote location and challenging terrain, the Plain of Jars continues to captivate the imagination of travelers seeking adventure, discovery, and cultural immersion in the heart of northern Laos. Whether marveling at the ancient stone jars, exploring nearby caves and waterfalls, or learning about the site's rich history and heritage, a visit to the Plain of Jars is sure to be a memorable and enlightening experience.

# Champasak: Ancient Temples and the Wat Phou Complex

Welcome to Champasak, a province in southern Laos renowned for its ancient temples and the magnificent Wat Phou complex. Situated on the banks of the Mekong River, Champasak is steeped in history and cultural significance, with a rich heritage that dates back over a thousand years. At the heart of Champasak lies the UNESCO World Heritage Site of Wat Phou, a sprawling temple complex that served as a center of worship and pilgrimage in ancient times.

The Wat Phou complex is believed to have been built during the 9th to 13th centuries, making it one of the oldest and most important archaeological sites in Laos. The temple complex is dedicated to the Hindu god Shiva and is laid out in a series of terraces and pavilions, culminating in a grand staircase that leads to a sanctuary at the summit. The temple's architecture is a blend of Khmer and Lao styles, with intricate carvings, bas-reliefs, and sculptures depicting Hindu deities, mythological creatures, and scenes from ancient epics.

One of the most iconic features of Wat Phou is its imposing central sanctuary, known as the prasat, which is flanked by two smaller pavilions and adorned with elaborate carvings and sculptures. The prasat is believed to have housed a linga, or phallic symbol representing the god Shiva, and served as a focal point for religious rituals and ceremonies.

In addition to its religious significance, Wat Phou also played a crucial role in the political and cultural life of the ancient Khmer Empire, serving as a center of royal power and authority. The temple complex was part of a network of Khmer sites that stretched across Southeast Asia, connecting Champasak to other major cities such as Angkor in present-day Cambodia.

Today, Wat Phou remains an important pilgrimage site for Buddhists and Hindus, who come to pay their respects and seek blessings at the sacred shrines and altars within the temple complex. The site is also a popular tourist destination, attracting visitors from around the world eager to explore its ancient ruins, learn about its history and significance, and admire its breathtaking natural surroundings.

In addition to Wat Phou, Champasak is also home to a wealth of other ancient temples and historical sites, including the pre-Angkorian temple of Vat Phou Asa and the ruined Khmer temple of Oum Muong. These temples offer further insights into the region's rich cultural heritage and architectural legacy, providing visitors with a fascinating glimpse into the ancient civilizations that once thrived in southern Laos.

Whether exploring the ancient ruins of Wat Phou, marveling at the intricate carvings and sculptures, or simply soaking in the serene beauty of the Mekong River, a visit to Champasak is sure to be a memorable and enriching experience for travelers seeking to uncover the hidden treasures of Laos.

# The 4000 Islands: Tranquility on the Mekong River

Welcome to the 4000 Islands, a serene and picturesque region nestled in the mighty Mekong River in southern Laos. As the name suggests, the 4000 Islands is comprised of numerous small islands scattered across the Mekong, creating a tranquil and idyllic landscape that is perfect for relaxation and rejuvenation.

The main islands in the 4000 Islands region are Don Det, Don Khon, and Don Khong, each offering its own unique charm and attractions for visitors to explore. Don Det and Don Khon are particularly popular among backpackers and budget travelers, with a laid-back atmosphere, affordable accommodation options, and plenty of opportunities for outdoor activities such as kayaking, tubing, and cycling.

One of the highlights of any visit to the 4000 Islands is the chance to witness the rare and elusive Irrawaddy dolphins that inhabit the waters of the Mekong River. These gentle creatures, known for their distinctive rounded heads and friendly demeanor, can often be spotted swimming and playing in the calm waters around Don Khon and Don Khong, providing visitors with a memorable wildlife encounter.

In addition to its natural beauty and abundant wildlife, the 4000 Islands is also steeped in history and cultural heritage, with a rich legacy that dates back centuries. Don Khon, in particular, is home to several historic sites, including the remnants of a French colonial-era railway and the picturesque Liphi Waterfalls, also known as the Somphamit Waterfalls, which served as a major obstacle for French colonialists attempting to navigate the Mekong River.

For those seeking a taste of local life and culture, the 4000 Islands offers plenty of opportunities to interact with the friendly and hospitable residents of the islands. Visitors can sample traditional Lao cuisine at local restaurants, visit traditional villages to learn about traditional crafts and customs, or simply relax in a hammock and soak in the laid-back vibe of island life.

Despite its growing popularity as a tourist destination, the 4000 Islands remains relatively undeveloped and unspoiled, offering visitors a chance to escape the hustle and bustle of modern life and reconnect with nature in a pristine and tranquil setting. Whether exploring its lush landscapes, spotting dolphins in the river, or simply enjoying the peaceful ambiance of island living, a visit to the 4000 Islands is sure to be a memorable and enriching experience for travelers seeking tranquility on the Mekong River.

# Exploring Laotian Arts and Crafts: Textiles, Silversmithing, and Woodwork

Welcome to the vibrant world of Laotian arts and crafts, where centuries-old traditions continue to thrive in the hands of skilled artisans and craftsmen. From intricate textiles and exquisite silversmithing to masterful woodwork and beyond, Laos boasts a rich and diverse artistic heritage that reflects the country's cultural richness and creativity.

One of the most celebrated forms of Laotian craftsmanship is textiles, which are renowned for their intricate designs, vibrant colors, and impeccable quality. Handwoven textiles have been an integral part of Laotian culture for centuries, with traditional techniques passed down from generation to generation. The most famous textile-producing regions in Laos include Luang Prabang, Xieng Khouang, and Savannakhet, where local artisans use traditional looms and natural dyes to create stunning fabrics, including silk, cotton, and hemp.

Silversmithing is another revered art form in Laos, with artisans producing intricate silver jewelry, decorative objects, and religious artifacts using traditional techniques handed down through the ages. Silverwork has deep cultural and spiritual significance in Laos, with many pieces featuring motifs inspired by Buddhist iconography, nature, and folklore. The city of Luang Prabang is particularly renowned for its silver craftsmanship, with skilled artisans producing everything from delicate filigree earrings to elaborate ceremonial objects.

Woodwork is also a cherished tradition in Laos, with artisans using locally sourced timber to create a wide range of objects, including furniture, sculptures, and architectural elements. The intricate carvings and detailed designs found in Laotian woodwork are a testament to the skill and craftsmanship of the country's artisans, who draw inspiration from nature, mythology, and religious symbolism. The town of Pakse, located in southern Laos, is known for its skilled woodworkers who produce intricately carved furniture and decorative items using traditional techniques.

In addition to textiles, silversmithing, and woodwork, Laos is also home to a wealth of other traditional crafts, including pottery, basket weaving, and papermaking. These crafts play a vital role in preserving cultural heritage, supporting local economies, and promoting sustainable livelihoods in rural communities across the country.

For visitors to Laos, exploring the world of Laotian arts and crafts offers a unique opportunity to connect with the country's rich cultural heritage and learn about the traditions and techniques that have been passed down through generations. Whether admiring the intricate patterns of a handwoven textile, marveling at the skill of a silversmith shaping molten metal, or appreciating the beauty of a finely carved wooden sculpture, the artistic traditions of Laos are sure to inspire and delight travelers from around the world.

# Traditional Music and Dance: Expressions of Laotian Identity

Welcome to the enchanting world of traditional music and dance in Laos, where centuries-old rhythms and movements continue to echo through the hearts and minds of the Laotian people. Music and dance are deeply ingrained in the cultural fabric of Laos, serving as powerful expressions of identity, spirituality, and community.

Laos boasts a rich and diverse musical heritage, with traditional instruments such as the khene, a bamboo mouth organ, and the pin, a three-stringed lute, playing a central role in both religious and secular contexts. The melodic sounds of these instruments, accompanied by rhythmic percussion and vocal harmonies, create a mesmerizing tapestry of sound that reflects the country's cultural diversity and artistic creativity.

One of the most iconic forms of traditional music in Laos is the mor lam, a genre of folk music that originated in the rural regions of northeastern Laos. Mor lam is characterized by its distinctive vocal style, which combines melodic singing with rhythmic chanting, accompanied by instruments such as the khene, drum, and cymbals. The lyrics of mor lam songs often reflect themes of love, nature, and everyday life, providing a glimpse into the hopes, dreams, and struggles of the Laotian people.

In addition to mor lam, Laos is also home to a variety of traditional dance forms, each with its own unique style, costumes, and movements. One of the most popular dance forms in Laos is the lam vong, a graceful and elegant dance performed at weddings, festivals, and other social gatherings. The dance is characterized by its slow and rhythmic movements, which are accompanied by traditional Lao music and often involve intricate hand gestures and footwork.

Another celebrated dance form in Laos is the ramvong, a lively and energetic dance performed in a circle by participants of all ages. The dance is often accompanied by live music, with musicians playing traditional instruments such as the khene and drum, and dancers moving in sync to the rhythmic beat. The ramvong is a popular form of social dance in Laos, bringing people together to celebrate special occasions and community events.

In addition to mor lam and traditional dance, Laos is also known for its vibrant festival culture, with religious and cultural celebrations held throughout the year to honor Buddhist traditions, harvest seasons, and ancestral spirits.

These festivals often feature colorful processions, elaborate costumes, music, dance, and rituals that reflect the country's rich cultural heritage and spiritual beliefs.

Overall, traditional music and dance are essential elements of Laotian identity, serving as powerful expressions of cultural pride, community cohesion, and spiritual connection. Whether performed at weddings, festivals, or everyday gatherings, these artistic traditions continue to play a central role in shaping the cultural landscape of Laos and enriching the lives of its people.

# The Legacy of the Ho Chi Minh Trail: History and Remembrance

Welcome to the enduring legacy of the Ho Chi Minh Trail, a historic route that played a pivotal role in the Vietnam War and continues to evoke memories of conflict, resilience, and perseverance in Laos. Stretching from North Vietnam through eastern Laos and into Cambodia, the Ho Chi Minh Trail served as a vital supply route for the North Vietnamese Army, allowing them to transport troops, weapons, and supplies to the front lines in South Vietnam.

The trail, named after the revolutionary leader Ho Chi Minh, was a complex network of roads, paths, and trails that traversed some of the most rugged and remote terrain in Southeast Asia. It was meticulously constructed and maintained by the North Vietnamese Army and the Viet Cong, who utilized a combination of manpower, ingenuity, and determination to overcome the formidable challenges posed by the region's dense forests, steep mountains, and unpredictable weather.

Despite facing relentless bombing campaigns by American forces, the Ho Chi Minh Trail remained operational throughout the Vietnam War, providing a lifeline for the communist forces fighting in South Vietnam. The trail's strategic importance was underscored by its ability to bypass conventional supply routes and evade detection by enemy forces, allowing the North Vietnamese Army to sustain their military operations and prolong the conflict. Today, the Ho Chi Minh Trail stands as a powerful symbol of Laos' wartime past and the enduring legacy of the Vietnam War. While much of the trail has been reclaimed by nature, remnants of its infrastructure, including bridges, bunkers, and supply depots, can still be found scattered throughout the countryside, serving as haunting reminders of the conflict that once ravaged the region.

In recent years, efforts have been made to preserve and commemorate the history of the Ho Chi Minh Trail, with museums, memorials, and historical sites dedicated to honoring the sacrifices made by those who fought and died along its rugged paths. These sites offer visitors a chance to learn about the trail's significance, explore its remnants, and pay tribute to the thousands of soldiers and civilians who lost their lives during the Vietnam War.

Despite the passage of time, the legacy of the Ho Chi Minh Trail continues to resonate deeply in Laos, shaping the country's collective memory and influencing its political, social, and cultural landscape. Whether viewed as a symbol of resistance and liberation or as a reminder of the devastation wrought by war, the Ho Chi Minh Trail remains an indelible part of Laos' history and identity, serving as a testament to the resilience and fortitude of its people in the face of adversity.

# Laos Today: Political Landscape and Contemporary Issues

Welcome to Laos today, where the political landscape and contemporary issues shape the country's present and future trajectory. Laos is a socialist republic, with a single-party political system dominated by the Lao People's Revolutionary Party (LPRP). The party has held power since 1975, following the communist revolution that ended the monarchy and established the Lao People's Democratic Republic.

The LPRP maintains tight control over the country's political institutions, including the government, military, and judiciary, exerting considerable influence over all aspects of governance and decision-making. While Laos has a constitution that enshrines certain rights and freedoms, including freedom of speech and assembly, these rights are often restricted in practice, with dissent and opposition discouraged and sometimes suppressed.

In recent years, Laos has undergone significant economic development and modernization, driven largely by foreign investment, infrastructure projects, and the expansion of industries such as mining, hydropower, and tourism. The government has pursued a policy of economic liberalization and market-oriented reforms, opening up the country to foreign trade and investment while striving to maintain political stability and social order.

Despite its economic progress, Laos faces a number of contemporary issues and challenges that threaten to undermine its development and stability. One of the most pressing issues is environmental degradation, particularly in rural areas where large-scale development projects, such as hydropower dams and mining operations, have led to deforestation, soil erosion, and pollution of waterways.

Another major challenge facing Laos is poverty and income inequality, with a significant portion of the population still living below the poverty line and lacking access to basic services such as healthcare, education, and clean water. Rural communities, in particular, face barriers to economic opportunity and social mobility, leading to disparities in living standards and quality of life.

Additionally, Laos is grappling with social issues such as drug trafficking, human trafficking, and corruption, which pose serious threats to public safety, human rights, and the rule of law. The government has implemented measures to address these, including strengthening law enforcement, enhancing border security, and promoting international cooperation, but progress has been slow and uneven.

In recent years, Laos has also faced criticism from human rights organizations and the international community over its treatment of political dissidents, activists, and minority groups. Freedom of expression and assembly are severely restricted, with individuals who speak out against the government often subject to harassment, intimidation, and arrest.

Overall, Laos today is a country at a crossroads, grappling with the challenges of modernization, economic development, and political stability while striving to address the needs and aspirations of its diverse population. The path forward is uncertain, but with continued efforts to promote transparency, accountability, and inclusive governance, Laos has the potential to overcome its challenges and build a brighter future for all its citizens.

# Sustainable Tourism in Laos: Balancing Development with Preservation

Welcome to the chapter on sustainable tourism in Laos, where the delicate balance between development and preservation is at the forefront of efforts to promote responsible travel and protect the country's natural and cultural heritage. As one of the fastest-growing sectors of the Lao economy, tourism has the potential to bring significant economic benefits to local communities while also fostering environmental conservation and cultural preservation.

Laos is blessed with abundant natural beauty, including lush forests, pristine rivers, and diverse wildlife, making it a popular destination for eco-tourism and adventure travel. The country's rich cultural heritage, with its ancient temples, traditional villages, and vibrant festivals, further adds to its appeal as a unique and authentic travel destination.

However, the rapid growth of tourism in Laos has also brought with it challenges and concerns, including environmental degradation, cultural commodification, and social disruption. Large-scale infrastructure projects, such as roads, airports, and hotels, have led to habitat loss, pollution, and disruption of local ecosystems, threatening the very resources that attract tourists to the country in the first place.

To address these challenges, the Lao government, in collaboration with local communities and international organizations, has taken steps to promote sustainable tourism practices and minimize the negative impacts of tourism on the environment and local culture. This includes implementing regulations and guidelines for responsible tourism, supporting community-based tourism initiatives, and investing in conservation efforts to protect natural and cultural heritage sites.

One example of sustainable tourism in Laos is the Nam Et-Phou Louey National Protected Area, which is home to a diverse range of wildlife, including the critically endangered Indochinese tiger. The Nam Et-Phou Louey Ecolodge, operated by local communities in partnership with conservation organizations, offers visitors the opportunity to experience the beauty of the protected area while supporting wildlife conservation and community development initiatives.

In addition to eco-tourism, Laos is also promoting cultural tourism as a way to preserve and celebrate its unique cultural heritage.

Traditional festivals, handicraft workshops, and homestay experiences allow visitors to immerse themselves in Lao culture, learn from local artisans and communities, and contribute to the preservation of traditional knowledge and skills.

Ultimately, sustainable tourism in Laos is about finding a balance between economic development and environmental conservation, between meeting the needs of tourists and respecting the rights and aspirations of local communities. By embracing principles of sustainability, stewardship, and respect for local culture and environment, Laos can ensure that tourism continues to be a positive force for economic growth, environmental protection, and cultural preservation for generations to come.

# Language and Communication: Navigating Lao for Travelers

Welcome to the chapter on language and communication in Laos, where understanding the basics of Lao can greatly enhance your travel experience in this beautiful country. Lao is the official language of Laos and is spoken by the majority of the population. It belongs to the Tai-Kadai language family and shares similarities with Thai, particularly in terms of vocabulary and grammar.

While Lao is the official language, there are also several minority languages spoken by ethnic groups throughout the country, including Hmong, Khmu, and Akha. English is increasingly spoken in urban areas and tourist destinations, particularly among younger generations and those working in the tourism industry. However, outside of major cities and tourist hubs, proficiency in English may be limited, so knowing some basic Lao phrases can be incredibly helpful for travelers.

Learning a few key phrases in Lao can go a long way in facilitating communication and building rapport with locals during your travels. Common greetings such as "sabaidee" (hello) and "khob chai" (thank you) are widely used and appreciated by Lao people. Other useful phrases include "koy pom pen yuu tee nai?" (where is the restroom?), "baw pen nyang" (no problem), and "lai lai" (slowly).

Lao is a tonal language, meaning that the tone or pitch of a word can change its meaning. There are six tones in Lao: high, mid, low, falling, rising, and short. Mastering the correct tones can be challenging for non-native speakers, but making an effort to pronounce words accurately will be greatly appreciated by locals.

In addition to spoken language, Lao also has its own script, which is derived from the ancient Brahmic script and is written from left to right. The Lao script is used primarily for formal writing, such as signage, newspapers, and official documents. While learning to read and write Lao may not be necessary for most travelers, being able to recognize some common words and phrases in the Lao script can be helpful for navigating menus, signs, and other written materials.

Overall, while English proficiency is increasing in Laos, particularly in urban areas, knowing some basic Lao phrases and understanding cultural norms around communication can greatly enhance your travel experience and help you connect more deeply with the local people and culture. So take the time to learn a few key phrases, practice your pronunciation, and embrace the opportunity to immerse yourself in the rich linguistic and cultural tapestry of Laos.

# Getting Around Laos: Transportation Tips and Travel Routes

Welcome to the chapter on getting around Laos, where we'll explore the various transportation options available to travelers in this diverse and enchanting country. Laos is known for its rugged terrain, scenic landscapes, and rich cultural heritage, making it an ideal destination for exploration and adventure. Whether you're navigating bustling cities, winding mountain roads, or tranquil rivers, there are plenty of ways to get around and experience all that Laos has to offer.

One of the most common and convenient modes of transportation in Laos is the bus. Buses operate on both short and long-distance routes, connecting major cities, towns, and tourist destinations across the country. While buses vary in terms of comfort and amenities, they offer an affordable and reliable way to travel between different regions of Laos. Most bus stations are centrally located and easily accessible, making it easy to hop on and off as you explore the country.

For those seeking a more immersive and scenic travel experience, traveling by boat along the

Mekong River is a popular option. The Mekong River, which flows through much of Laos, offers stunning views of lush landscapes, traditional villages, and historic temples as you cruise along its meandering waters. Riverboats and ferries operate on various routes, including the popular journey between Luang Prabang and Huay Xai, near the border with Thailand.

For travelers looking to explore remote and off-the-beaten-path destinations, renting a motorbike or bicycle can be a great way to get around. Motorbikes are widely available for rent in major cities and tourist areas, offering the freedom to explore at your own pace and venture off the main roads. Bicycle rentals are also available and are a popular choice for exploring smaller towns, rural villages, and scenic countryside.

In addition to buses, boats, and bikes, travelers in Laos can also make use of taxis, tuk-tuks, and songthaews (shared minibusses) for shorter journeys and local transportation. Taxis are common in major cities such as Vientiane and Luang Prabang, while tuk-tuks and songthaews are popular in smaller towns and rural areas. Negotiating fares in advance is common practice, so be sure to agree on a price before starting your journey.

Another unique transportation option in Laos is the "jumbo" or "sawngthaew," which are modified pickup trucks with covered seating in the back. These vehicles operate on fixed routes and can be flagged down like a bus, making them a convenient and affordable way to travel short distances within cities and towns.

Overall, getting around Laos offers a chance to experience the country's diverse landscapes, vibrant culture, and warm hospitality firsthand. Whether you're cruising down the Mekong River, exploring ancient temples by motorbike, or hopping on a local bus to a nearby village, there's no shortage of ways to discover the wonders of Laos and create unforgettable memories along the way.

# Accommodation Options: From Guesthouses to Luxury Resorts

Welcome to the chapter on accommodation options in Laos, where we'll explore the wide range of choices available to travelers seeking a comfortable and memorable stay in this captivating country. From cozy guesthouses and budget-friendly hostels to luxurious resorts and boutique hotels, Laos offers something for every taste, budget, and travel style.

For budget-conscious travelers, guesthouses and hostels are popular accommodation options that provide affordable and often charming places to stay. Guesthouses are typically family-run establishments offering basic amenities such as private or shared rooms, communal bathrooms, and common areas where guests can relax and socialize. Hostels, on the other hand, cater more to backpackers and budget travelers, offering dormitory-style accommodations with shared facilities and a lively atmosphere. In addition to guesthouses and hostels, Laos also offers a wide range of mid-range hotels and resorts that provide comfortable accommodations at reasonable prices. These hotels often feature amenities such as private rooms with ensuite bathrooms, air conditioning, Wi-Fi, and on-site restaurants or cafes. Many mid-range hotels also offer additional services such as tour booking, airport transfers, and laundry facilities to enhance the guest experience. For travelers seeking a more luxurious and indulgent experience, Laos boasts a number of high-end resorts and boutique hotels that offer world-class amenities, personalized service, and stunning surroundings. These resorts are often located in scenic locations such as riverbanks, mountainsides, or lush forests, providing a tranquil and idyllic setting for relaxation and rejuvenation. Amenities at luxury resorts may include spacious villas or suites, gourmet dining options, spa and wellness facilities, and recreational activities such as swimming pools, tennis courts, and guided excursions. In recent years, Laos has also seen the rise of eco-friendly and sustainable accommodation options, including eco-lodges, homestays, and community-based tourism initiatives. These accommodations offer travelers the opportunity to immerse themselves in local culture, support sustainable tourism practices, and minimize their environmental footprint while exploring the natural beauty and cultural richness of Laos. Overall, whether you're a budget traveler looking for a cozy guesthouse, a mid-range traveler seeking comfort and convenience, or a luxury traveler in search of indulgence and relaxation, Laos has accommodation options to suit every preference and budget. So whether you're planning a backpacking adventure through remote villages, a romantic getaway along the Mekong River, or a family vacation in the heart of the city, you're sure to find the perfect place to call home during your stay in Laos.

# Cultural Etiquette: Dos and Don'ts for Visitors

Welcome to the chapter on cultural etiquette in Laos, where we'll delve into the dos and don'ts for visitors to ensure a respectful and enjoyable experience in this diverse and culturally rich country. Laos is known for its warm hospitality, deeply rooted traditions, and strong sense of community, and understanding and respecting local customs and etiquette is key to fostering positive interactions and building meaningful connections with the people of Laos.

One of the most important aspects of cultural etiquette in Laos is showing respect for elders and authority figures. In Lao culture, age and hierarchy are highly valued, and it is customary to address older individuals and those in positions of authority with deference and respect. This may include using formal titles such as "kun" (Mr.), "nang" (Mrs.), or "aaj" (Miss), followed by the person's name when addressing them.

Another important cultural etiquette in Laos is the concept of "face," which refers to maintaining harmony and avoiding conflict or embarrassment in social interactions. As such, it is considered impolite to raise your voice, show anger or frustration, or publicly criticize or embarrass someone, as this can cause loss of face for both parties involved. Instead, it is better to remain calm, patient, and respectful, even in challenging situations.

When visiting temples and religious sites in Laos, it is important to dress modestly and respectfully, covering your shoulders, knees, and cleavage, and removing your shoes before entering sacred spaces. It is also customary to show reverence and respect for Buddhist images, statues, and artifacts by refraining from touching them or posing for photos with them, unless given explicit permission to do so.

In addition to respecting religious customs, visitors to Laos should also be mindful of local customs and traditions related to food and dining. In Lao culture, it is customary to eat with your right hand, using your fingers to pick up food from shared dishes. It is also polite to wait for the host or eldest person at the table to begin eating before you start, and to offer compliments to the cook or host for the meal.

When interacting with locals in Laos, it is important to greet people with a smile and a respectful "sabaidee" (hello) or "sabaidee baw" (hello, how are you?) to show friendliness and goodwill. It is also customary to show gratitude and appreciation for acts of kindness or hospitality by saying "khob chai" (thank you) or "khob chai lai lai" (thank you very much).

Overall, by observing these cultural dos and don'ts, visitors to Laos can show respect for local customs and traditions, foster positive interactions with the people of Laos, and create meaningful and memorable experiences during their travels in this enchanting country. So embrace the opportunity to learn about and immerse yourself in Lao culture, and enjoy the warm hospitality and rich cultural heritage that awaits you in Laos.

# Exploring Laotian Markets: Vibrant Hubs of Commerce and Culture

Welcome to the chapter on exploring Laotian markets, where we'll dive into the vibrant hubs of commerce and culture that characterize the bustling marketplaces of Laos. Markets play a central role in daily life in Laos, serving as not only places to buy and sell goods but also as social and cultural gathering spaces where locals and visitors alike come together to exchange news, share stories, and celebrate community.

Laos is home to a wide variety of markets, ranging from sprawling outdoor bazaars to bustling indoor markets and night markets that come alive after sunset. Each market offers its own unique blend of sights, sounds, and smells, reflecting the diversity of the country's cultural heritage and culinary traditions.

One of the most iconic and atmospheric markets in Laos is the morning market in Luang Prabang, where vendors set up stalls along narrow alleyways selling everything from fresh produce and spices to handmade crafts and souvenirs. The market is a feast for the senses, with the aroma of sizzling street food wafting through the air and the colorful displays of fruits, vegetables, and textiles catching the eye of passersby. In addition to the morning market in Luang Prabang, visitors to Laos can also explore the vibrant night markets that spring up in cities and towns across the country. These markets are a kaleidoscope of colors and flavors, with vendors selling a wide array of street food, handicrafts, clothing, and jewelry under the glow of twinkling lanterns and neon lights.

Another must-visit market in Laos is the Talat Sao (Morning Market) in Vientiane, the capital city, which offers a dizzying array of goods ranging from traditional Lao textiles and handicrafts to electronics, clothing, and household items. The market is a popular destination for both locals and tourists, with vendors haggling over prices and shoppers browsing the stalls in search of bargains and treasures. In addition to the larger markets, Laos is also home to countless smaller village markets and roadside stalls where farmers and artisans sell their wares directly to consumers. These markets offer a glimpse into rural life in Laos and provide an opportunity to sample local specialties such as sticky rice, grilled meats, and fresh fruits and vegetables.

Overall, exploring Laotian markets is a feast for the senses and a window into the rich tapestry of culture, tradition, and commerce that defines life in Laos. So whether you're hunting for souvenirs, sampling street food, or simply soaking up the sights and sounds of daily life, be sure to make time to wander through the vibrant markets of Laos during your travels in this enchanting country.

# Laotian Handicrafts: Souvenirs and Their Cultural Significance

Welcome to the chapter on Laotian handicrafts, where we'll explore the rich tradition of artisanal craftsmanship and the cultural significance of souvenirs in Laos. Handicrafts play an integral role in Lao culture, serving as expressions of creativity, heritage, and identity, and providing a livelihood for countless artisans and their families across the country.

One of the most iconic handicrafts in Laos is traditional silk weaving, which has been practiced for centuries by skilled artisans using techniques passed down through generations. Lao silk is renowned for its fine quality, intricate designs, and vibrant colors, and is used to create a wide range of textiles, including scarves, shawls, sarongs, and ceremonial garments. Visitors to Laos can often witness the ancient art of silk weaving firsthand at weaving villages and workshops, where skilled weavers work tirelessly at their looms, transforming raw silk into exquisite fabrics.

In addition to silk weaving, Laos is also known for its traditional handicrafts such as bamboo and rattan weaving, pottery, woodcarving, and silver and goldsmithing. Each of these crafts has its own unique history, techniques, and cultural significance, and reflects the diverse ethnic traditions and artistic heritage of the Lao people.

Bamboo and rattan weaving, for example, are integral to Lao daily life, with artisans skillfully crafting a wide range of household items such as baskets, mats, and furniture from these natural materials. Pottery-making is another ancient craft in Laos, with artisans using traditional techniques to create functional and decorative ceramic ware, including pots, bowls, and jars, adorned with intricate designs and patterns.

Woodcarving is another popular handicraft in Laos, with artisans carving intricate designs and motifs into wood to create sculptures, furniture, and decorative items such as masks and figurines. Silver and goldsmithing, meanwhile, are highly valued crafts in Laos, with artisans using traditional techniques to create stunning jewelry and ornaments, often featuring intricate filigree work and motifs inspired by nature and Buddhist symbolism.

In addition to their artistic and aesthetic value, Laotian handicrafts also hold cultural significance as symbols of identity, tradition, and heritage. Many handicrafts are deeply rooted in Lao religious and cultural practices, with motifs and designs often inspired by Buddhist teachings, mythology, and folklore. By purchasing and supporting local handicrafts, travelers can not only take home beautiful and unique souvenirs but also contribute to the preservation of Lao cultural heritage and the livelihoods of local artisans.

Overall, Laotian handicrafts are a testament to the creativity, skill, and cultural richness of the Lao people, and exploring the vibrant world of Lao handicrafts is an essential part of any visit to this enchanting country. So whether you're browsing the bustling markets of Luang Prabang, visiting remote weaving villages in the countryside, or admiring the intricate designs of silver jewelry in Vientiane, be sure to take the time to appreciate the beauty and significance of Laotian handicrafts during your travels in Laos.

# Laotian Textiles: Weaving Traditions and Techniques

Welcome to the fascinating world of Laotian textiles, where centuries-old weaving traditions and intricate techniques come together to create some of the most exquisite fabrics in the world. Textiles play a central role in Lao culture, serving not only as practical items for clothing and household use but also as symbols of cultural identity, social status, and spiritual beliefs.

One of the most iconic textile traditions in Laos is silk weaving, which has been practiced for generations by skilled artisans using traditional hand looms. Lao silk is renowned for its fine quality, lustrous sheen, and rich colors, and is prized by collectors and connoisseurs around the world. Silk weaving is a labor-intensive process that requires patience, skill, and meticulous attention to detail, from spinning raw silk threads to dyeing them with natural plant-based dyes and weaving them into intricate patterns and designs.

The art of silk weaving is passed down through generations within families and communities, with knowledge and techniques handed down from mothers to daughters and from master weavers to apprentices. Many weaving villages

81

in Laos are known for their unique styles and patterns, with each village producing its own distinct variations of silk textiles, including ikat, brocade, and supplementary weft designs.

Ikat, or "mat mee" in Lao, is a traditional weaving technique in which yarns are dyed before weaving to create intricate patterns and designs. The process involves tying and dyeing the yarns in specific patterns to create a resist effect, resulting in bold and vibrant designs that are characteristic of Lao ikat textiles. Brocade weaving, meanwhile, involves the use of supplementary weft threads to create raised or textured patterns on the fabric, adding depth and dimension to the finished textile.

In addition to silk weaving, Laos is also known for its cotton textiles, which are woven using both traditional hand looms and modern techniques. Cotton weaving is practiced by many ethnic groups in Laos, with each group producing its own distinctive styles and patterns. Cotton textiles are often adorned with intricate motifs and designs inspired by nature, mythology, and Buddhist symbolism, reflecting the cultural heritage and artistic traditions of the Lao people.

Whether silk or cotton, traditional Laotian textiles are treasured for their beauty, craftsmanship, and cultural significance, and are often used for special occasions such as weddings, festivals, and religious ceremonies. In recent years, there has been a renewed interest in traditional textile techniques and a growing recognition of the importance of preserving and promoting Lao textile heritage for future generations.

Overall, Laotian textiles are a testament to the creativity, skill, and cultural richness of the Lao people, and exploring the world of Lao textile traditions is an essential part of any visit to this enchanting country. So whether you're admiring the intricate patterns of a handwoven silk scarf in a bustling market or learning about traditional weaving techniques in a remote village, take the time to appreciate the beauty and significance of Laotian textiles during your travels in Laos.

# Laotian Cuisine: A Culinary Journey Through the Regions

Welcome to the flavorful world of Laotian cuisine, where a culinary journey through the regions offers a tantalizing array of dishes that reflect the country's diverse landscapes, cultural heritage, and culinary traditions. From the fragrant aromas of lemongrass and galangal in northern Lao soups to the fiery spices of southern Lao curries, each region of Laos offers its own unique flavors, ingredients, and cooking techniques that will delight and inspire adventurous food lovers.

In northern Laos, where the terrain is mountainous and the climate cooler, traditional dishes are often hearty and warming, with an emphasis on freshwater fish, game meats, and foraged ingredients such as bamboo shoots, wild mushrooms, and herbs. One of the most iconic dishes of northern Lao cuisine is "kaeng nor mai," a spicy bamboo shoot soup flavored with lemongrass, lime leaves, and chilies, served with sticky rice and fresh herbs.

In central Laos, where the landscape is characterized by lush forests and fertile valleys, traditional dishes are influenced by both northern and southern Lao culinary traditions, resulting in a diverse and eclectic cuisine that celebrates the bounty of the land and the river. Staples such as "larb," a spicy minced meat salad, and "mok pa," a steamed fish curry wrapped in banana leaves, are popular dishes enjoyed throughout the region.

In southern Laos, where the Mekong River flows and the climate is tropical, traditional dishes are often spicy and aromatic, with an emphasis on fresh herbs, vegetables, and seafood. One of the most beloved dishes of southern Lao cuisine is "tam mak hoong," a fiery papaya salad made with shredded green papaya, chilies, tomatoes, and peanuts, pounded together in a mortar and pestle and served with sticky rice and grilled meats.

Throughout Laos, sticky rice is a staple food and is enjoyed with almost every meal, often served in small woven baskets and eaten with the hands. Lao cuisine also features a wide variety of fermented foods and condiments, including "jaew," a spicy dipping sauce made with chilies, fish sauce, and herbs, and "padek," a pungent fermented fish paste that adds depth and complexity to many dishes.

In addition to traditional Lao dishes, Laos is also influenced by the culinary traditions of neighboring countries such as Thailand, Vietnam, and China, resulting in a fusion of flavors and ingredients that adds depth and diversity to Lao cuisine. Whether you're savoring a bowl of "khao piak sen," a hearty noodle soup, in Luang Prabang, or indulging in "or lam," a rich and savory stew, in Pakse, a culinary journey through the regions of Laos is sure to delight the senses and leave you craving more.

# Lao Street Food: Delicacies and Must-Try Dishes

Welcome to the vibrant world of Lao street food, where the bustling streets come alive with the sights, sounds, and aromas of savory delights and culinary treasures waiting to be discovered. Street food plays a central role in Lao gastronomy, offering a convenient and affordable way for locals and visitors alike to experience the diverse flavors and textures of Lao cuisine in a casual and convivial atmosphere.

One of the most iconic and beloved street foods in Laos is "khao jee pate," a delicious sandwich made with French baguette bread, filled with a generous spread of pate, mayonnaise, lettuce, cilantro, and sometimes sliced ham or grilled meats. This fusion of French and Lao flavors is a popular snack or quick meal enjoyed by people of all ages throughout the country.

Another must-try street food in Laos is "moo ping," or grilled pork skewers, which are marinated in a flavorful mixture of garlic, soy sauce, oyster sauce, and spices before being grilled over hot coals until tender and caramelized. These juicy and fragrant skewers are often served with sticky rice and a spicy dipping sauce made with chili and lime, making them a favorite street food snack or appetizer.

For those craving something spicy and aromatic, "larb" is a quintessential Lao street food dish that packs a punch of flavor. Larb is a spicy minced meat salad made with ground meat (often chicken, pork, or beef), fish sauce, lime juice, toasted rice powder, chili flakes, and fresh herbs such as mint, cilantro, and green onions. This vibrant and zesty dish is typically served with fresh vegetables and sticky rice, and is a staple of Lao street food stalls and markets.

In addition to savory dishes, Lao street food also offers a tantalizing array of sweet treats and desserts to satisfy your sweet tooth. One popular dessert is "khao nom kok," or coconut pancakes, which are small round pancakes made with coconut milk, rice flour, and sugar, cooked in a special pan until golden brown and crispy on the outside and soft and tender on the inside. These delightful bite-sized treats are often enjoyed as a snack or dessert, and are best enjoyed hot off the griddle.

Whether you're exploring the bustling night markets of Luang Prabang, sampling savory snacks from roadside vendors in Vientiane, or savoring sweet treats from food carts in Pakse, Lao street food offers a culinary adventure that is sure to tantalize your taste buds and leave you craving more. So embrace the sights, sounds, and flavors of Lao street food culture, and immerse yourself in the vibrant and diverse culinary landscape of this enchanting country.

# The Flavors of Laos: From Sticky Rice to Spicy Papaya Salad

Welcome to the chapter that delves into the delightful flavors of Laos, where every dish tells a story of tradition, culture, and the rich tapestry of ingredients that make up the country's vibrant culinary landscape. From the ubiquitous staple of sticky rice to the fiery kick of spicy papaya salad, each flavor evokes the essence of Laos and its diverse culinary heritage.

Let's start with sticky rice, the cornerstone of Lao cuisine and a staple food that is enjoyed with almost every meal. Known locally as "khao niew," sticky rice is steamed and served in small woven baskets, with diners using their fingers to roll and scoop the rice into bite-sized portions. This unique method of eating reflects the communal and convivial nature of Lao dining culture and is a symbol of hospitality and generosity.

Moving on to the realm of savory delights, Lao cuisine is renowned for its bold and complex flavors, with dishes often characterized by the use of aromatic herbs, pungent fish sauce, and fiery chilies. One of the most iconic Lao dishes is "larb," a spicy minced meat salad made with ground meat (typically chicken, pork, or beef), fish sauce, lime juice, toasted rice powder, and fresh herbs such as mint, cilantro, and green onions. Larb is a celebration of bold flavors and textures, with each bite bursting with zesty freshness and a hint of heat.

Another beloved dish that embodies the flavors of Laos is "tam mak hoong," or spicy papaya salad. Made with shredded green papaya, tomatoes, chilies, lime juice, fish sauce, and peanuts, this refreshing salad is a symphony of sweet, sour, salty, and spicy flavors that dance on the palate. Tam mak hoong is often served alongside grilled meats, sticky rice, and other traditional Lao dishes, and is a favorite street food snack enjoyed throughout the country.

No exploration of Lao flavors would be complete without a mention of "mok pa," a traditional dish of steamed fish curry wrapped in banana leaves. Made with fresh river fish, coconut milk, herbs, and spices, mok pa is a fragrant and flavorful dish that highlights the bounty of the Mekong River and the lush landscapes of Laos. The fish is wrapped in banana leaves and steamed until tender, allowing the flavors to meld together and create a dish that is both comforting and aromatic.

Finally, we come to dessert, where the sweet flavors of Laos take center stage. One popular sweet treat is "khao nom kok," or coconut pancakes, which are made with coconut milk, rice flour, and sugar, cooked until golden brown and crispy on the outside and soft and tender on the inside. These bite-sized delights are often enjoyed as a snack or dessert, and are a delightful way to end a meal on a sweet note.

In conclusion, the flavors of Laos are as diverse and dynamic as the landscapes that inspire them, with each dish offering a unique and tantalizing glimpse into the culinary heritage of this enchanting country. So whether you're savoring the simplicity of sticky rice or indulging in the bold flavors of larb and spicy papaya salad, let your taste buds be your guide on a culinary journey through the flavors of Laos.

# The Mekong River: Lifeline of Laos and Its People

Welcome to the chapter dedicated to the mighty Mekong River, the lifeline of Laos and its people. Flowing through six countries in Southeast Asia, the Mekong holds immense significance for Laos, shaping its landscape, economy, culture, and way of life.

Originating from the Tibetan Plateau, the Mekong River winds its way through China, Myanmar, Thailand, Laos, Cambodia, and Vietnam, covering a distance of over 4,900 kilometers before emptying into the South China Sea. In Laos, the Mekong stretches for about 1,835 kilometers, serving as a vital artery that sustains communities along its banks and beyond.

The Mekong River plays a crucial role in the daily lives of millions of people in Laos, providing a source of livelihood through fishing, agriculture, and transportation. Fishing is particularly important, with the Mekong supporting a rich diversity of fish species that are integral to the diets and economies of many communities. Fishermen rely on traditional fishing methods such as cast nets, bamboo traps, and gill nets to catch fish, using techniques that have been passed down through generations.

In addition to fishing, the Mekong River also supports agriculture along its fertile floodplains, where farmers cultivate rice, vegetables, fruits, and other crops. The river's annual flood cycle replenishes the soil with nutrients, making it ideal for agriculture and supporting the livelihoods of countless rural communities. In recent years, hydropower development along the Mekong has raised concerns about its impact on fish populations, river ecosystems, and the livelihoods of people who depend on the river for their survival.

Beyond its economic importance, the Mekong River holds deep cultural and spiritual significance for the people of Laos. It is often referred to as the "Mother of Waters" and is associated with legends, folklore, and religious beliefs. Many Lao communities hold ceremonies and festivals to honor the river and seek its blessings for a bountiful harvest, good fortune, and protection from harm.

The Mekong River also serves as a vital transportation route, connecting remote villages and towns with urban centers and markets. Traditional wooden boats, known as "long boats" or "sam pans," ply the river's waters, carrying passengers, cargo, and goods to and from the bustling riverfront markets that line its banks. In recent years, the construction of bridges and improved road networks has facilitated greater connectivity and trade between communities along the Mekong River.

Overall, the Mekong River is much more than just a body of water—it is the lifeblood of Laos, sustaining communities, ecosystems, and cultures across the country. Its significance extends far beyond its physical boundaries, shaping the identity, heritage, and resilience of the Lao people for generations to come. So as you journey through Laos, take a moment to appreciate the majesty and magnificence of the Mekong River, and the vital role it plays in the fabric of Lao society.

# Exploring Laos by Bike: Cycling Adventures and Routes

Welcome to the exhilarating world of exploring Laos by bike, where adventurous travelers can embark on cycling adventures that take them off the beaten path and into the heart of this enchanting country. With its stunning landscapes, diverse terrain, and rich cultural heritage, Laos offers endless opportunities for cyclists of all levels to pedal their way through scenic routes, remote villages, and ancient temples.

One of the most popular cycling routes in Laos is the "Mekong River Loop," which follows the course of the mighty Mekong River as it winds its way through lush countryside, sleepy villages, and bustling towns. Starting in the capital city of Vientiane, cyclists can pedal northward along the river, passing through picturesque landscapes of rice paddies, limestone cliffs, and traditional Lao stilt houses. Along the way, they can stop to explore ancient temples, riverside markets, and scenic viewpoints that offer panoramic views of the Mekong River and the surrounding countryside. For those seeking a more challenging adventure, the "Bolaven Plateau Loop" offers a thrilling cycling experience through the rugged highlands of southern Laos. Starting in Pakse, cyclists can traverse winding mountain roads, lush rainforests, and cascading waterfalls as they make their way through the scenic Bolaven Plateau.

Along the way, they can visit traditional Lao villages, coffee plantations, and ethnic minority communities, immersing themselves in the rich cultural heritage and natural beauty of the region.

For the ultimate cycling adventure, cyclists can embark on the "Luang Namtha Loop," a multi-day journey through the remote and pristine landscapes of northern Laos. Starting in the town of Luang Namtha, cyclists can pedal through dense jungles, rolling hills, and serene river valleys as they explore remote villages, ethnic minority markets, and ancient ruins along the way. With its challenging terrain and breathtaking scenery, the Luang Namtha Loop offers a truly unforgettable cycling experience for adventurous travelers.

In addition to these iconic cycling routes, Laos also offers a variety of shorter day trips and half-day excursions for cyclists of all abilities. From leisurely rides along scenic river paths to adrenaline-pumping downhill descents through rugged mountain terrain, there's something for everyone to enjoy on two wheels in Laos.

Whether you're a seasoned cyclist looking for an epic adventure or a casual rider seeking a leisurely pedal through the countryside, exploring Laos by bike offers a unique and immersive way to experience the beauty and culture of this captivating country. So grab your helmet, hop on your saddle, and get ready to embark on the cycling adventure of a lifetime in Laos.

# Trekking in Laos: Trails Through Lush Forests and Remote Villages.

Welcome to the chapter dedicated to trekking in Laos, where adventurous souls can embark on exhilarating journeys through lush forests, rugged mountains, and remote villages, immersing themselves in the natural beauty and cultural richness of this enchanting country. With its diverse landscapes, pristine wilderness, and warm hospitality, Laos offers endless opportunities for trekkers of all levels to explore off-the-beaten-path trails and experience the untamed beauty of Southeast Asia.

One of the most popular trekking destinations in Laos is the northern province of Luang Namtha, home to the Nam Ha National Protected Area and a network of scenic trekking trails that wind through dense jungles, misty mountains, and traditional hill tribe villages. Trekkers can embark on multi-day hikes through the pristine wilderness, camping under the stars and experiencing the rich biodiversity of the region, including rare wildlife such as gibbons, elephants, and Asiatic black bears.

In southern Laos, the Bolaven Plateau offers another exciting trekking experience, with trails that lead through verdant coffee plantations, thundering waterfalls, and lush rainforests.

Trekkers can explore remote villages inhabited by ethnic minority groups such as the Laven, Alak, and Katu, learning about their traditional ways of life and cultural customs along the way. The Bolaven Plateau is also home to the famous Tad Fane waterfall, a stunning natural wonder that plunges over 100 meters into a deep gorge, providing a breathtaking backdrop for trekkers to enjoy.

For those seeking a more challenging adventure, the remote mountains of northern Laos offer rugged terrain and pristine wilderness for trekkers to explore. The Phou Louey National Protected Area, also known as the "Forever Mountain," is home to some of the country's highest peaks, densest forests, and most remote villages. Trekkers can embark on multi-day expeditions to summit Phou Louey and other peaks, camping in the wilderness and experiencing the thrill of true adventure in one of the last remaining wilderness areas in Southeast Asia.

In addition to these iconic trekking destinations, Laos also offers a variety of shorter day hikes and half-day excursions for trekkers of all abilities. From leisurely strolls through scenic river valleys to challenging ascents up steep mountain slopes, there's something for everyone to enjoy on the trekking trails of Laos.

So whether you're an experienced trekker seeking a wilderness adventure or a casual hiker looking to explore the natural beauty and cultural heritage of Laos, trekking in this captivating country offers an unforgettable journey through some of the most breathtaking landscapes and remote villages in Southeast Asia. So lace up your hiking boots, pack your backpack, and get ready to experience the thrill of trekking in Laos.

# Waterfalls of Laos: Natural Wonders Waiting to Be Discovered

Welcome to the captivating chapter that unveils the natural wonders of Laos—the breathtaking waterfalls that cascade through lush forests, carve their way through rugged landscapes, and beckon travelers with their mesmerizing beauty. From towering cascades to hidden gems tucked away in remote corners of the country, Laos is home to an array of spectacular waterfalls just waiting to be discovered and explored.

One of the most iconic waterfalls in Laos is the magnificent Kuang Si Falls, located near the city of Luang Prabang in the north. This multi-tiered waterfall tumbles over limestone cliffs into turquoise pools below, creating a picture-perfect oasis amidst the verdant jungle. Visitors can swim in the crystal-clear waters, hike along scenic trails, and marvel at the cascading beauty of the falls from various viewpoints.

Further south, the Tad Sae Waterfall offers another enchanting retreat for nature lovers. Situated near the town of Luang Prabang, this picturesque waterfall is surrounded by lush vegetation and can be reached by boat or trekking through the forest. Visitors can swim in the cool waters, relax in the shade of the surrounding trees, and enjoy a picnic amidst the tranquil sounds of nature.

In southern Laos, the majestic Tad Fane Waterfall steals the spotlight with its dramatic twin streams plunging over 100 meters into a deep gorge below. Located in the Bolaven Plateau, this impressive natural wonder is surrounded by dense forests and coffee plantations, making it a popular stop for trekkers and nature enthusiasts exploring the region.

For those seeking off-the-beaten-path adventures, the remote province of Xieng Khouang is home to the mysterious Tad Xe Waterfall, also known as the "Waterfall of Spirits." Accessible only by boat or trekking through dense jungle, this hidden gem offers a secluded and tranquil escape for intrepid travelers looking to immerse themselves in the raw beauty of Laos.

These are just a few examples of the many stunning waterfalls that dot the landscape of Laos, each with its own unique charm and allure. Whether you're seeking adventure, relaxation, or simply a moment of awe-inspiring natural beauty, the waterfalls of Laos are sure to leave a lasting impression and create memories that will last a lifetime. So pack your swimsuit, lace up your hiking boots, and get ready to explore the natural wonders of Laos—one waterfall at a time.

# Birdwatching in Laos: A Paradise for Avian Enthusiasts

Welcome to the vibrant world of birdwatching in Laos, where enthusiasts are treated to an avian paradise brimming with diverse species, stunning habitats, and rich biodiversity. Nestled in the heart of Southeast Asia, Laos offers birdwatchers an unparalleled opportunity to explore lush forests, winding rivers, and expansive wetlands in search of rare and exotic birds that call this diverse landscape home.

With its varied ecosystems and strategic location along major migratory routes, Laos boasts over 900 species of birds, making it a haven for both resident and migratory avifauna. From colorful songbirds to majestic raptors, the birdlife of Laos is as diverse as it is captivating, offering endless opportunities for birdwatchers to observe and photograph some of the world's most beautiful and elusive feathered creatures.

One of the premier birdwatching destinations in Laos is the Nam Et-Phou Louey National Protected Area, located in the northern part of the country. This vast wilderness area is home to a rich array of bird species, including the critically endangered white-winged duck, the elusive green peafowl, and the majestic crested kingfisher. Birdwatchers can explore the park's dense forests, winding rivers, and pristine wetlands in search of

101

these and other rare and endemic species, all while enjoying the breathtaking scenery and tranquility of the natural surroundings.

In southern Laos, the wetlands of the Mekong River offer another excellent birdwatching opportunity, with thousands of migratory waterfowl congregating along the river's banks during the winter months. Birdwatchers can spot a wide variety of species, including herons, egrets, ducks, and shorebirds, as they forage for food and roost in the tranquil waters of the Mekong Delta.

For those seeking high-altitude adventures, the mountainous regions of northern Laos provide an ideal habitat for a number of specialized bird species, including the elusive white-eared night heron, the beautiful black-throated sunbird, and the striking scarlet-faced liocichla. Birdwatchers can trek through remote forests and alpine meadows in search of these and other highland species, enjoying the challenge of spotting birds in their natural habitat and the thrill of discovering new and rare species.

Whether you're a seasoned birdwatcher or a novice enthusiast, Laos offers a wealth of opportunities to connect with nature and experience the beauty and wonder of its avian inhabitants. So grab your binoculars, pack your field guide, and get ready to embark on an unforgettable birdwatching adventure in the Land of a Million Elephants.

# Conservation Efforts: Protecting Laos' Natural Heritage

In this chapter, we delve into the crucial efforts aimed at conserving and preserving the natural heritage of Laos, a country blessed with an abundance of biodiversity and ecological wonders. As the demand for natural resources and development pressures increase, the need to safeguard Laos' unique ecosystems and wildlife becomes more urgent than ever.

One of the primary focuses of conservation efforts in Laos is the protection of its extensive network of national parks and protected areas. These areas, which cover approximately 14% of the country's land area, serve as vital refuges for endangered species, critical habitats, and important ecosystems. Through partnerships with local communities, government agencies, and international organizations, these protected areas are managed and monitored to ensure the long-term sustainability of Laos' natural heritage. Another key aspect of conservation in Laos is the protection of its diverse wildlife species, many of which are threatened by habitat loss, poaching, and illegal wildlife trade. Efforts to combat these threats include the establishment of wildlife sanctuaries, the implementation of anti-poaching patrols, and the enforcement of laws and regulations aimed at curbing illegal wildlife trafficking. Additionally, community-based conservation initiatives empower local communities to become stewards of their natural resources and partners in conservation efforts. In recent years, Laos has also made significant strides in promoting sustainable tourism practices that minimize the negative impacts on the environment and local communities. Eco-tourism initiatives, such as responsible trekking tours, wildlife watching excursions, and community-based homestays, provide travelers with unique opportunities to experience Laos' natural beauty while supporting conservation efforts and sustainable development. Furthermore, environmental education and awareness-raising campaigns play a crucial role in fostering a culture of conservation among the people of Laos. Through school programs, community workshops, and public outreach events, efforts are underway to educate individuals about the importance of biodiversity, the threats facing the environment, and the actions they can take to protect and preserve their natural heritage for future generations. Overall, conservation efforts in Laos are multifaceted and involve a wide range of stakeholders working together to address the complex challenges facing the country's natural environment. By prioritizing sustainable development, promoting community engagement, and implementing effective conservation strategies, Laos is striving to protect its rich natural heritage and ensure a sustainable future for generations to come.

# Exploring Laotian Temples: Spiritual Journeys Through Time

Welcome to the enchanting world of Laotian temples, where ancient traditions, rich history, and spiritual reverence converge to create a truly captivating experience for visitors. Throughout the verdant landscapes and bustling cities of Laos, temples, or "wats" as they are locally known, stand as timeless symbols of the country's cultural heritage and religious devotion.

Among the most renowned temples in Laos is the UNESCO World Heritage Site of Luang Prabang, where over 30 temples dot the historic cityscape, each with its own unique architectural style and cultural significance. From the majestic golden spires of Wat Xieng Thong to the intricate carvings of Wat Mai, these temples offer a glimpse into the rich artistic and spiritual traditions of Laos' royal capital.

In the capital city of Vientiane, visitors can explore the iconic Pha That Luang, a towering golden stupa that is considered the national symbol of Laos. Dating back to the 16th century, this sacred monument is a focal point for Buddhist worship and pilgrimage, attracting devotees from across the country and around the world.

Further south, the ancient temple complex of Wat Phou in Champasak province provides a fascinating glimpse into Laos' pre-Buddhist history and Khmer heritage. Built on the slopes of a sacred mountain, Wat Phou is one of the oldest archaeological sites in Laos and is dedicated to the Hindu god Shiva, showcasing intricate stone carvings, ancient shrines, and panoramic views of the surrounding countryside.

In addition to these iconic sites, Laos is home to countless other temples, both large and small, each offering its own unique atmosphere and spiritual significance. From remote hilltop retreats to bustling urban centers, temples play a central role in the daily lives of the Lao people, serving as places of worship, meditation, and community gatherings.

Visitors to Laos' temples are often struck by the serene beauty, spiritual tranquility, and profound sense of history that permeates these sacred spaces. Whether you're admiring the ornate architecture, participating in a traditional Buddhist ceremony, or simply soaking in the peaceful ambiance, exploring Laotian temples is a journey of discovery, reflection, and reverence that leaves a lasting impression on the soul.

# Festivals of Laos: Celebrating Tradition and Community

Welcome to the vibrant tapestry of Laotian festivals, where tradition, culture, and community come together in a colorful celebration of life. Throughout the year, Laos plays host to a dazzling array of festivals and events that reflect the rich diversity of its people, their beliefs, and their way of life.

One of the most eagerly anticipated festivals in Laos is the annual celebration of Pi Mai Lao, or Lao New Year, which takes place in mid-April and marks the beginning of the traditional Lao lunar calendar. Lasting for three days, Pi Mai Lao is a time of joyous revelry, with streets filled with music, dance, and water fights as locals and visitors alike come together to cleanse away the old year and welcome in the new.

Another highlight of the Laotian festival calendar is Boun Bang Fai, or the Rocket Festival, which is held in May to mark the beginning of the rainy season and encourage plentiful rainfall for the crops. During this lively event, colorful handmade rockets are launched into the sky in a spirited competition, accompanied by traditional music, dancing, and feasting.

For those with a penchant for cultural spectacle, the That Luang Festival in Vientiane offers a mesmerizing display of Buddhist devotion and pageantry. Held in November at the iconic Pha That Luang stupa, this festival attracts pilgrims from across Laos who come to pay homage to the sacred relic housed within the stupa and participate in colorful processions, religious ceremonies, and merit-making activities.

In addition to these major festivals, Laos is also home to a wide variety of regional and ethnic celebrations that showcase the unique traditions and customs of its diverse population. From the Hmong New Year festivities in the northern highlands to the boat racing festivals along the Mekong River, there is always something to celebrate and experience in Laos.

Whether you're witnessing the spectacle of a grand procession, sampling the flavors of traditional Lao cuisine, or joining in the joyous dancing and merrymaking, the festivals of Laos offer an unforgettable glimpse into the heart and soul of this fascinating country. So come, immerse yourself in the spirit of celebration, and discover the magic of Laotian festivals for yourself.

# Laos Through the Lens: Photography Tips and Inspiration

Welcome to the chapter where we explore Laos through the lens of a camera, capturing the beauty, culture, and spirit of this enchanting land. Whether you're an amateur photographer or a seasoned pro, Laos offers endless opportunities for stunning photographs that will inspire and captivate.

One of the first things you'll notice when photographing Laos is the incredible diversity of landscapes, from lush jungles and mist-shrouded mountains to serene rivers and ancient temples. Each region of the country has its own unique charm and character, providing a wealth of subjects to photograph and explore.

In Luang Prabang, you'll find yourself immersed in a UNESCO World Heritage Site filled with ornate temples, traditional architecture, and bustling markets. The soft morning light filtering through the trees, the vibrant colors of the saffron-robed monks, and the serene atmosphere of the alms-giving ceremony make for unforgettable photo opportunities.

In Vientiane, the capital city, you'll discover a blend of colonial-era buildings, bustling streets, and riverside promenades. From the iconic

Patuxai monument to the serene beauty of the Mekong River at sunset, there's no shortage of photogenic spots to capture the essence of urban life in Laos.

Venture into the countryside, and you'll encounter a landscape dotted with picturesque villages, terraced rice fields, and hidden waterfalls. Whether you're trekking through the rugged mountains of northern Laos or cruising along the tranquil waters of the Nam Ou River, you'll be treated to breathtaking vistas and cultural encounters that beg to be photographed.

When photographing people in Laos, it's important to approach with respect and sensitivity. Many Lao people are happy to have their picture taken, but always ask permission first and be mindful of cultural sensitivities. Portraits of monks, farmers, artisans, and children can offer a glimpse into the everyday lives and traditions of the Lao people, capturing moments of genuine emotion and connection.

For nature lovers, Laos is a paradise of biodiversity, with dense forests, pristine rivers, and rare wildlife species waiting to be discovered. Whether you're photographing exotic birds in the Nam Et-Phou Louey National Protected Area or capturing the vibrant colors of tropical flowers in the Bolaven Plateau, the natural beauty of Laos is sure to inspire and awe.

In terms of photography equipment, a DSLR or mirrorless camera with a versatile lens (such as a zoom lens or prime lens) is ideal for capturing a wide range of subjects and compositions. Don't forget to bring plenty of memory cards, spare batteries, and a sturdy tripod for those long exposure shots or group portraits.

Lastly, don't be afraid to experiment with different techniques and perspectives to add visual interest to your photos. Try shooting from different angles, playing with light and shadow, and experimenting with composition and framing to create unique and compelling images that tell the story of your journey through Laos.

In the end, photography is not just about capturing images; it's about capturing moments, emotions, and memories that will last a lifetime. So grab your camera, explore the beauty of Laos, and let your creativity soar as you document the wonders of this remarkable country through your own unique lens.

# Planning Your Trip: Practical Advice and Resources

Welcome to the chapter where we dive into the practicalities of planning your trip to Laos. Whether you're a first-time visitor or a seasoned traveler, careful planning can make all the difference in ensuring a smooth and enjoyable experience in this captivating country.

First things first, let's talk about when to visit Laos. The best time to visit depends on your preferences and interests. The dry season, from November to April, is generally considered the peak tourist season, with pleasant weather, clear skies, and optimal conditions for outdoor activities and sightseeing. However, this is also the busiest time of year, so be prepared for larger crowds and higher prices.

If you prefer to avoid the crowds and don't mind the occasional rain shower, the wet season, from May to October, can be a great time to visit. During this time, the countryside comes alive with lush greenery, waterfalls are at their most spectacular, and the rice paddies are a vibrant shade of green. Just be aware that some areas may be prone to flooding, and certain activities, such as trekking and river travel, may be limited.

Next, let's talk about getting to Laos. The most common way to enter the country is by air, with international airports in Vientiane, Luang Prabang, and Pakse serving as major gateways for travelers. Several airlines operate flights to Laos from neighboring countries such as Thailand, Vietnam, Cambodia, and China, making it relatively easy to reach from various parts of the world.

For those already in Southeast Asia, traveling to Laos overland is also an option. Bus services connect Laos with neighboring countries such as Thailand, Vietnam, and Cambodia, offering affordable and convenient transportation options for budget-conscious travelers. Additionally, Laos is accessible via boat from Thailand along the Mekong River, providing a scenic and adventurous route into the country.

Once you've arrived in Laos, it's time to think about accommodation. From budget-friendly guesthouses and backpacker hostels to luxurious resorts and boutique hotels, Laos offers a wide range of accommodation options to suit every taste and budget. In popular tourist destinations such as Luang Prabang and Vientiane, it's a good idea to book accommodation in advance, especially during peak season when availability can be limited.

When it comes to getting around Laos, there are several transportation options to choose from. Buses, minivans, and tuk-tuks are the most common modes of public transportation, providing affordable and convenient ways to travel between cities and towns. For longer distances, domestic flights are available between major cities, although they can be more expensive than overland travel.

For those looking to explore off the beaten path, renting a motorbike or bicycle can be a great way to experience the countryside at your own pace. Just be sure to exercise caution and adhere to local traffic laws, as road conditions in rural areas can be rough and traffic can be chaotic.

Finally, before embarking on your journey to Laos, it's important to do your research and familiarize yourself with local customs, culture, and etiquette. Learning a few basic phrases in Lao, the official language of Laos, can go a long way in helping you connect with locals and navigate everyday situations.

Additionally, be sure to check the latest travel advisories and health recommendations from reputable sources such as the Centers for Disease Control and Prevention (CDC) and the World Health Organization (WHO). It's also a good idea to have travel insurance that covers medical emergencies, trip cancellations, and other unexpected events.

By taking the time to plan ahead and make informed decisions, you can ensure a safe, enjoyable, and memorable trip to Laos that will leave you with a lifetime of cherished memories. So pack your bags, prepare for adventure, and get ready to experience the beauty and hospitality of this remarkable country firsthand.

# Epilogue

As we come to the end of our journey through the wonders of Laos, it's time to reflect on the experiences we've shared and the memories we've made along the way. From the misty mountains of Luang Prabang to the bustling streets of Vientiane, from the tranquil waters of the Mekong River to the ancient temples of Champasak, Laos has captured our hearts and left an indelible mark on our souls.

Throughout this book, we've delved into the rich tapestry of Laotian culture, explored its diverse landscapes, and marveled at its fascinating history. We've learned about the ancient kingdoms that once ruled these lands, the colonial powers that left their mark, and the resilient spirit of the Lao people who have endured and thrived through it all.

We've savored the flavors of Laotian cuisine, from spicy papaya salad to sticky rice and grilled meats, and discovered the vibrant markets where locals gather to buy and sell fresh produce, handicrafts, and other goods. We've marveled at the intricate craftsmanship of Laotian textiles, admired the beauty of its traditional music and dance, and gained a deeper understanding of the spiritual significance of Buddhism in everyday life. We've explored the natural wonders of Laos, from its lush jungles and cascading waterfalls to its diverse

116

wildlife and pristine national parks. We've embarked on outdoor adventures, from trekking through remote villages to birdwatching in secluded forests, and experienced the thrill of encountering rare and endangered species in their natural habitats.

But perhaps most importantly, we've connected with the people of Laos, whose warmth, generosity, and hospitality have touched our hearts and left a lasting impression. Whether sharing a meal with a local family, learning traditional crafts from skilled artisans, or simply exchanging smiles and greetings with strangers along the way, we've experienced firsthand the true spirit of Laotian hospitality.

As we bid farewell to this enchanting land, let us carry with us the memories of our time here and the lessons we've learned along the way. Let us continue to cherish and celebrate the beauty and diversity of Laos, and strive to preserve and protect its natural and cultural heritage for future generations to enjoy.

And so, as we close the final chapter of our journey, let us remember that the spirit of Laos will always remain in our hearts, beckoning us to return again someday to explore its wonders anew. Until then, may the memories we've made here continue to inspire and enrich our lives, reminding us of the beauty and wonder that awaits us in every corner of the world.

Made in the USA
Las Vegas, NV
15 February 2025

18179237R00066